30-day Devotional Journal for Women
Preparing for Their Kingdom Marriage Promise

Weather the Wait

Volume I

JANAY WELLS

Published by Janay Wells

Editing and graphic design by Karen Bowlding

Cover Image by Torriphoto

ISBN: 978-0-578-96814-8

Dedication

"Blessed is she who has believed that the Lord
would fulfill his promises to her!"

Luke 1:45, NIV

I dedicate this book to all the women that have a kingdom marriage promise from God. To all the women that have felt that it would never come, weary in the wait, and trying to stand on God's Word. I created this devotional journal because I found others going through the same issues, facing the same fears, and wanting to strengthen their relationship with God.

Many of these topics I have personally walked out, and I received encouragement from those who have been weathering the wait longer or have faced other obstacles. This devotional journal is designed to help you reflect, pray, and press into each topic. It is designed for you to have conversations with God and be receptive to what He wants to speak to you. I prayed for you as I wrote this devotional book what God wants to say through me to you. He is changing broken hearts. Sadness and disappointment will not be your portion. What God has started in you; He is faithful to complete. Don't give up on His promises! God will always come through! We are weathering the wait together!

Acknowledgments

"Being confident of this, that he who began a good work in you will carry it on to completion until the day of Christ Jesus."

- Philippians 1:6 (NLT)

Dear God: thank you for trusting me with this assignment. Thank you for giving me vision and helping me to run with it even when I didn't want to write this book. Thank you for leading me with every Scripture, encouragement, prayer, and poem. Thank you for using me and this book for your purpose and glory. Thank you for seeing me, loving me, and believing in me! I thank you that the lives of hundreds of women will be touched and uplifted through this book. I thank you that this will continue to grow and move forward as you see it.

-

Dear YouTube Family: thank you to every subscriber who came across my videos and supported me. I have prayed for you before you even arrived on my YouTube channel.

Thank you for purchasing my first book and I pray that it helps you in your walk. Continue to be amazing and fulfill God's purpose for your life. No matter what it looks like, keep believing in God because he will never let you down!

-

Dear Ms. Jackie: I met you at the altar at I5 Church. I was desperate for a move from God. You have been like a mother-figure to me. You have encouraged me in this journey through so many ways. You kept it real with me and weren't afraid to correct me. You were always leading me back to God and making sure I heard from Him first. You found ways to help me better understand my tests and trials. You often remind me of how far I have grown in the past year. You encourage me to keep pushing forward and to lean into God's presence.

-

Dear Ms. Kerra: I met you at the altar at I5 Church. We have since had countless hours talking on the phone. You have prayed for me many times when I couldn't pray for myself. You were there to lift my heart when I called you while crying. You encouraged me to keep pressing forward in my business and book. You envisioned me writing this book before I did. God gave you a word and I didn't tell you that I wanted to write a devotional journal. I just didn't know how to start. You knew the colors and where this will go next. Thank you for encouraging me and walking with me. You are a true friend. Thank you for always supporting me!

-

Dr. Rhonda Mayes: your videos on YouTube have really comforted and encouraged me. Many times, I didn't realize that others were going through the same things. Your videos have been confirming and many times I started laughing just because of the title. Most of the time, God was already speaking to my heart what you later posted. I just knew that God was reassuring me through your videos and giving me peace even in the middle.

-

Dear Jeannette Bruno: I found you on YouTube. I have always appreciated your videos and how authentic you are. Thank you for being a beacon of light to us all. Thank you for your obedience and faith. Thank you for writing an encouragement to be included in this book. It is such a beautiful message and I know it will uplift many who read it. Continue to follow God's plan and purpose for your life. You are inspiring many!

-

Mrs. Karen: thank you, for helping me to create my first book! Thank you for your patience and dedication over the months of trying to produce my book. This has turned out better than I could imagine. Thank you for being a part of the process. I can't wait to see what my next books become with you on my team.

-

Thank you to many other people that I may have not mentioned who have encouraged and supported me through the process.

Preface

I am on a journey of trusting God in this specific promise in my life. I struggled with fully letting go and letting God be God. I struggled with fear of rejection, worry, fear, etc. I am on this journey in community with other women that are going through the same issues. Some have been waiting for years and years, some have lost hope in ever finding a mate, and some that struggle with the process of the wait. I realized that I wasn't alone, and many others were facing the same battles and struggles.

Sometimes, when we are not in community with other believers, we feel isolated. We can feel that we are the only ones going through issues and we don't know how to overcome them. We may struggle with accepting this call on our life and believing that we are worthy of receiving a kingdom marriage. We may still have soul wounds, soul ties, and hurts that need to be healed. We need to be delivered from them. We may feel like God favors others more than us and that we are overlooked by God. The good news is that we are not overlooked by God, nor forgotten!

I struggled with patience in this journey. We all know the saying: "Don't pray for patience?" Well, I did, and God has been testing me in this area and continues to do so. I am a prophetic dreamer; it's just how God communicates with me. He revealed things to me, and I didn't always understand it because my faith was being tested. It didn't look like what God said, and doubt and fear tried to creep up on me to steal what God planted in me. If the enemy can plant seeds of doubt, fear, and mistrust into your mind for it to take root, he can try to make you miss what God is really revealing to you. I'm starting to just let go and fully surrender control in how, what, where, and when it should happen. This has been hard for me because I like to know the plan, the details, and feel like I have a sense of control. However, God doesn't operate like this, and it wouldn't require faith if He showed us everything. I spent a lot of time praying, fasting, conversing with God, worshipping, etc. I've experienced a lot of opposition, but I thank God that it is all coming full circle. He knows our needs and the proper time to give us our promised kingdom marriage. This isn't just any marriage, but a kingdom marriage! This will display God's purpose and glory on the Earth. Because of this, we must be in alignment with God and rest in what He is doing in the waiting period. Sometimes we are waiting on God to move when He really is waiting on us to do the necessary work while in the waiting period. When we do the necessary work, God can elevate us to a new level and territory that He wants us to have.

Opening Prayer

Dear God, I thank every person that is reading this. I pray that it will bless and bring them hope. I pray for a breakthrough in their lives. I pray that they know who they are in you. They are not forgotten, and, in your timing, you will bring everything full circle. You will make their kingdom marriage happen in your timing and in your way. I thank you God for your ordained purpose in their lives. I thank God for speaking to them and guiding them. I thank you that as they go through this devotional journal, they will draw closer to you. I thank you that you are close to the broken-hearted and those that are crushed in spirit. I thank you for being our heavenly Father. You love and meet us right where we are. So, Father God, I thank you for seeing the needs of your people. You're giving them peace and understanding for every test and trial. We recognize you as sovereign Lord. We ask that you have your way in our lives. In Jesus' mighty name, amen.

As You Weather the Wait

As you are weathering the wait, God is preparing you and your mate
You may be looking for this and that, but He knows the best traits
You may feel overlooked or forgotten, but don't, God is never late.
As you are waiting, don't settle, God knows your wedding date

Opinions of others may start to feel like a heavy weight
Put your trust in Him and not in others, He is the one that knows your fate
Look to Him for directions, He is making your crooked places straight
Forgive those who have hurt you, you may have felt like bait, but don't harbor hate.

Obedience to the Lord is crucial, you get to choose, this is not up for debate.
Before you even know it, what you have been waiting for will open like a floodgate
His timing, not ours, He is not slow to keeping His promises, He is not going at our rate.
He knows your heart's desires, watch the promises unfold, He is the one that will create
He knew you before you were in your mother's womb, your qualities are innate

You may feel pressure, just like a pregnant woman, it's
10 centimeters to dilate
Just like labor, you may not feel like you can endure, but
keep pushing, the promises are great
God sees you and loves you, continue honoring Him as
you weather the wait

Table of Contents

Day 1

Wife in Waiting

"He who finds a wife finds a good thing and receives favor from the Lord."

Proverbs 18:22, NIV

For those who have received their marriage promise from the Lord, understand you are a wife. You are a part of the bride of Christ and God has chosen you. In Isaiah 54: 5, it states, "For your Maker is your husband—the Lord Almighty is his name—." We must understand that we are loved and chosen by God. We must first be faithful to Him, and He will release us to the man of God he has for us. We must understand: "He who finds a wife finds a good thing and receives favor from the Lord," (Proverbs 18:22). We don't have to go searching and trying to make our marriage promise happen on our own. While we are wives-in-waiting, there is work to do and we must be focused on our kingdom assignment. The Lord will have a joint kingdom assignment for his purpose and glory when we become one with our spouse. The word favor in Hebrew means grace. Our kingdom marriage will have the proper grace it needs when we do it His way. Many of us may look at the stories or highlights of others and want to be in their place. For example, being married, but understanding that there is a necessary process, and it doesn't always look pretty.

If you desire a kingdom marriage, you must be willing to let God do it His way and for His purpose on the Earth. You may feel like you have been waiting and waiting, and it seems like the promise will never come. However, if God has you waiting, trust that He knows what He is doing. It is a calling to be a wife, and God will be entrusting you to submit to Him and walk in agreement with your future spouse. When the man of God finds you, he will find you with the character of a wife. When you two unite, the favor and grace will be evident in each other's lives.

Nugget of Wisdom (NOW)

Do the necessary work while you are a wife in waiting. You will see later why the waiting period was vital.

Activation

Read Proverbs 31. Think about the qualities of the Proverbs 31 woman.

Reflect

What qualities do you think a wife should have? What qualities do you possess and what qualities would you like to have?

What is your view about the waiting period? How are you feeling right about being a wife-in-waiting?

What is some of the necessary work you must do before your kingdom marriage?

Pray

Father God, I thank you that you are my husband before you release me to my Earthly husband. I thank you that you know my needs and are here to help me along the journey. I thank you for pruning things off me that you know I should no longer have. I thank you for replacing those things with your character and your heart. Thank you for shaping and molding me for who you want me to be. I thank you for checking my heart and making it pure. I thank you for giving me grace in every season. Help me to be content in knowing that you know the right time for me to get married. I thank you for currently working on me and working on my future husband. I thank you God that at the appointed time, it shall not delay. Help me to cling to you more and to know that you are my first love and priority. In Jesus' mighty name, amen.

Day 2

Worthy of Love

"We love, because he first loved us."

1 John 4:19, NIV

I have had a difficult time in trusting the process because of my past hurts and disappointments. I was always fearful that I would be in a cycle of being rejected by the men I found interesting and adored by the men I didn't feel the same way about. I had fears of always being the one to put in more effort and time. I knew God gave me a big heart and He wanted me to pour out the love He had given me. I was giving, but not receiving. Sometimes, I subconsciously gave what I was hoping to get in return to feel validated or worthy of love. I didn't want to get the bottom of the barrel or the short end of the stick.

The reflection I had of myself wasn't the same as God's reflection. I had fears of abandonment and often struggled with the spirit of rejection. I tried to earn or perform to get God's love, and it was displayed in my relationships with people. I realized how much God loves me and how He is always pursuing me. I'm worthy of being poured into, loved, and pursued. Sometimes, based on the views we have of ourselves, we project it onto God and others. We may be upset at God or feel like He doesn't want to bless us. Somehow, we may feel unworthy of the blessing or like we will mess it up. We may not feel qualified to receive a kingdom marriage promise because of our past mistakes.

Thankfully, God is a redeemer, and He is faithful to forgive us once we repent. Oftentimes, we are holding onto things that God has forgiven and doesn't remember. You may be facing these same heart and spirit issues, but remember, you are a daughter of the Most High king. God loves you and He wants the absolute best for you.

Now

Receive God's love for you and watch how that love will overflow in your life.

Activation

Ask God how you can embrace His love for you. Ask what you can do to view yourself in the way that He sees you. Say out loud: "God chose me, God loves me, and God is enough for me. I'm worthy of being loved and loving others. Today, I receive God's love."

Reflect

How would you describe your relationship with God? How do you think He sees you?

____

____

____

____

What internal issues have you faced in giving and/or receiving love with God and with others?

____

____

____

____

In what ways are you working on overcoming these issues or can work on these issues?

____

____

____

____

Pray

Father God, I thank you for loving and embracing me. I thank you for reminding me of your everlasting love that never runs out. I thank you for calling me as a wife and helping me to continue to walk out the calling. I thank you that you are healing any soul wounds, soul ties, and other trauma I may have experienced. I thank you for healing any brokenness and for making me whole. I thank you for helping me to overcome anything that is standing in my way. Thank you for giving me the grace and the strength to carry out the current assignments you have placed on me. Thank you for choosing to love me and to be good to me. Thank you for valuing me and treasuring me. In Jesus' mighty name, amen.

Day 3

What Time is it?

"For everything there is a season, and a time for every matter under heaven: a time to be born, and a time to die; a time to plant, and a time to pluck up what is planted; a time to kill, and a time to heal; a time to break down, and a time to build up; a time to weep, and a time to laugh; a time to mourn, and a time to dance; a time to cast away stones, and a time to gather stones together; a time to embrace, and a time to refrain from embracing; a time to seek, and a time to lose; a time to keep, and a time to cast away; a time to tear, and a time to sew; a time to keep silence, and a time to speak; a time to love, and a time to hate; a time for war, and a time for peace."

Ecclesiastes 3: 1-8, ESV

Sometimes we feel like God is taking too long or we wonder when our marriage promise will be fulfilled. For everything there is a time and season. Sometimes we may get worked up trying to make something happen in our timing. Trust that God knows the right time to connect you both. You may be in a season of friendship, courtship, or maybe in a season when you feel lonely. No matter what season you are in, God is working on you and the other person.

Sometimes, we are ready, but not the other or vice versa. We can become frustrated when rushing the season, we are currently in or not fully embracing what God has for us now. "This vision is for a future time. It describes the end, and it will be fulfilled. If it seems slow in coming, wait patiently, for it will surely take place, it will not be delayed," (Habakkuk 2:3, NLT). We must weather the season we are in, even if we feel like there are delays. In the end, it will come to pass. Make sure you know what season it is and learn to embrace it. We can become frustrated when we are praying for our marriage promise out of season. Sometimes the answer is still yes, just not yet. We must make sure we are discerning the season. We must remember to "not awaken love until the time is right," (Song of Solomon 8:4, NLT). Right now, I'm in my building season, and working on the many projects the Lord has trusted me with. Seek the Lord on the timing for everything and focus on what He has you doing right now. The right man will come at the appointed time.

Now

When it's your time, it is your time, and there is nothing that can stop it.

Activation

Ask God what time it is for you in current season. Ask him what He expects of you in this season.

Reflect

What season are you currently in relating to your marriage promise?

____

____

____

____

What emotions have you been feeling in this season?

____

____

____

____

What is it that God is desiring of you and what are you desiring of God in this season?

____

____

____

____

Pray

Father God, I pray for discernment to know the time and season for my kingdom marriage. I pray that you would open my heart and spirit to clearly hear you. I pray to stay planted where you have me, to not go ahead of you and not behind you. I don't want to awaken love before it's time. Give me strength to wait for the proper time and to not grow weary in well doing. I give to you my disappointment, frustration, anxiety, and loneliness. I release any false burdens and responsibilities that you have not placed on me. I freely give you everything I have, withholding nothing. I cast my cares and anxieties onto you for you care for me. Thank you for teaching me what you want to grow in me this season. I thank you for pruning anything that is not like you off me in this season. I will walk in obedience and continue to follow your instructions. I won't get weary. I won't faint. I will keep being faithful in this season. You're always a faithful God, and your purposes shall be fulfilled in my life. In Jesus' mighty name, amen.

Day 4

Hidden

"A wife of noble character who can find? She is worth far more than rubies."

Proverbs 31:10, NIV

There were many times when I felt hidden. Sometimes I wondered where he would find me or when. Sometimes I felt like I was hidden for the right one, but all the wrong men kept finding me and it was frustrating. Sometimes we may even wonder how we are going to meet our future husband. For some of us, we may not really go out or feel like we get noticed by men. God knows where you are and where he is. God is hiding you, and that man must seek God just to find you.

For some, you are hidden in plain sight; that person may be in front of you. Scripture says, "Who can find a virtuous wife? For her worth *is* far above rubies," (Proverbs 31:10-31). Gems are hidden, and it often requires intense work to find. This person will be able to see the value you carry and add to your worth, not depreciate from your value. Trust in the right time and place, God will connect the two of you.

Now

You are hidden because you are meant to be discovered.

Activation

Have a conversation with God on the qualities that He sees in you.

Reflect

Do you feel like you have been hidden?

When your future spouse finds you, what qualities will he see?

How have you trusted God with Him hiding you and how have you been feeling about that?

Pray

Father God, thank you for hiding me. Thank you that the man that you have for me will have to seek your heart to find me. Thank you, God, for renewing and refining me. Help me to recognize the people that are not connected to your purpose and destiny for my life. Help me to walk away from anyone that may be trying to hinder or block the plans you have for me. Help me to recognize the purpose in the relationships I have now. Help me to nurture the current relationships I have with people. Help me to continue to be hidden until it is the proper time for me to be discovered.

I thank you God that the one you have for me will see the light I carry. I thank you God that there is no competition. I thank God that he will see many noble women, but he will see that I surpass them all. I thank you that he will be able to recognize who I am in due season. I thank you God for protecting his heart from any hurts. I pray that he will be mindful of who is in his circle. I pray that we continue to guard our hearts and watch what we speak. I pray that we follow your perfect will and everything that is not in your perfect alignment, be aligned right now. In Jesus' mighty name, amen.

Day 5

Lord Order His Steps to Find Me

"The steps of a man are established by the Lord, when he delights in his way."

Psalm 37:23, ESV

Dear God, you have been writing on the tablet of my heart
In moments like these I know we will never part
You have been speaking and speaking, even supernaturally
God, I know you will fulfill this not my way but extraordinarily
Sometimes I ponder and even start to question
But I know that you're the God of signs, miracles, and wonders
Thinking of all the possible reasons, I feel like I'm close to my due season
Does he see me or does he not, Lord I will put my trust in you, even when there aren't many clues
My faith has waived time and time, but I can hear you saying the promise is still mine.
You know the very beginning from the end
So many feelings and emotions have started to blend
Maybe it's both of our hearts that still must mend
There will be a special event we will both have to attend

It feels like a movie that keeps on buffering, patience, and longsuffering
These are the fruits that you are growing in me
Laying my worries at your feet and letting them be, you are the God who is perfect to the tee
Trying to work on this counseling degree, knowing that my faith is like a spiritual key
Even in these moments, I know it's your glory that I will see
In you I'm free and as I agree to your will that you have for me
Submit to God, resist the devil, and he shall flee
Your promises are yes and amen, that is a guarantee
You have given me supernatural vision, you have already graced this mission
Kingdom assignments are at hand, I will follow your commands, in righteousness I will stand
For you're getting ready to make it expand, it's okay if I don't fully understand, you are the God who makes things grand
I will just chill because I want your perfect will
I will stand strong; you say sing unto me a new song
For it is your purpose that I desire
I know that you are taking me higher
I can feel your Holy Spirit Fire
God it's you, who I admire
I will do the work you require, for you are my heavenly supplier

It doesn't matter what the enemy will conspire
Strength and resilience are what I will acquire
Is he sleeping or is he awake, thinking about how much time will this take
I will continue to cultivate the things you want me to make
Like a cake, I guess some things take longer to bake
The Lord says that he is near, there is no need to fear
So, dry your tears because the promise is here
He has already shifted things into gear, you will see it crystal clear
So let God steer and get ready to cheer, this is still your year
Like Job, I will come out of this fire refined as Gold
You are still writing the story before it's even told
I won't shy away; you have trusted me to be bold
In the meantime, I will be seeking your face
Your word is like the solid base, I know that I don't have to chase
I know in your presence there is plenty of space, You are fulfilling this case
I look around and all I can see is your grace, surely, I will finish this race.

I wrote this poem in October 2020. I sat down, and the Lord wanted to download a poem to me. I don't write poems often, but before I knew it, I created this poem. Many of you, including myself, have wondered or even worried about how the man God has for us will find us. Some of you may be thinking, "I don't even go out" or "There's no godly men out there." First, when you are doing what the Lord has asked you to do, he will find you working. You don't have to do anything extra or go searching in places where you think you will be found. It says, "His steps are ordered by the Lord."

When you are positioned where God has you, you don't have to do anything extra or flaunt yourself to get his attention. When the man of God is focusing on his assignment and when he is instructed by the Lord, his steps will cross paths with your steps. I remember, God showed me a dream when I was following God's instructions and so was my future husband and we were getting ready to cross paths. It wasn't anything extra that I did or he did, but God positioned us both at the right place and time.

I once heard Jerry Flowers say, "Favor is married to obedience." When you are obedient to the Lord, you will find yourself in the favorable places He wants you to be. Trust at the right time and place, you will meet. Also, be open to God surprising you. It may not be in the way you expect. Some of you are expecting to meet the in church. You may meet him at school, the library, or even online. Take the limits off God. He wants to do it His way and at His time. Most of the time it will be at the time and place you least expect, so let God be God. He knows best. Don't try to make things happen in your own strength. If you want God to get the glory, then get out of God's way!

now

He will find you right where you are positioned to be. Make sure you are receptive to the Holy Spirit.

Activation

Express to God that you trust Him despite what you see. Talk with God about your feelings and this waiting process. Ask God what He wants to do through you in the waiting process. Think of any mentalities or attitudes that need to be adjusted in this time.

Reflect

Do you trust God's divine timing and intervention regarding your kingdom marriage?

____

____

____

____

In what ways have you tried to put yourself out there to be seen? Did it work?

____

____

____

____

How will you surrender your way and time to the Lord? What do you need to repent for or be reminded of?

____

____

____

____

Pray

Father God, I thank you for preparing me to meet the one you desire for me. I thank you that you are doing a good work in me as you are doing with him. God, help me to be patient in awaiting him to arrive. Help me to not settle out of my impatience and to be led by the Holy Spirit. I thank you that you are ordering his steps to find me. I thank you that in due season he will recognize and know who I am. I thank you God that in our meeting, your glory will be revealed.

I understand that the man of God that you have for me will love and accept me for me. I thank you that he is praying for me as well and is following your directions. I ask that you remove any hindrances and barriers that may come in the way of us meeting or moving forward. I ask that any connections that are not from you be severed. Give me the strength to walk away from men who don't honor me or value me. My desire is to be obedient in what you have asked of me. Help me to not focus on the wait, but to be focused on what you desire of me in this season. I thank you God that he is coming. I thank you God that our hearts are preparing for each other and to be centered with you. In Jesus' mighty name, amen.

Day 6

Who's Your Director?

"My sheep hear my voice, and I know them, and they follow me."

John 10:27, ESV

After some conversations with a couple of people, I realized that I shouldn't have shared what God had shown me. Before I knew it, I had more doubt and confusion after those conversations. I saw the consequences of following their guidance. Be careful about who you share information and revelation, whether it's through his word, dreams, and visions with other people. This makes room for others to speak their own opinions and thus cause more doubt and confusion. If God says to wait, then wait, even if someone tells you to give up on that person. If God says to let that person go, don't negotiate. God sees what you don't see. Let them go.

Be careful of people who say you should just give up because it's taking too long. Who are they to judge because of how long it's taking? In the Bible there are many promises that God fulfilled that took a long time—Sarah and Abraham, Joseph, Hannah, and more. God is on his time (Kairos) not man's time (Chronos). If you have godly counsel, they will point you back to God. Be careful of those who say, "Thus saith the Lord...," and don't point you back to His Word. Be careful of familiar spirits that may try to get to you through others. You may have received some prophetic words and tested the spirit. Those should confirm what God has already spoken to you. Many of the words my accountability partners have prophetically spoken over my life matched with the information God already told me without me previously telling them. The more time you spend with God, the more you will know His voice and be able to distinguish what is not His voice. Don't indulge in too much outside noise because it can cloud what the Lord is speaking to you. We should want to read our Bibles because it's a conversation with God. We should be in communion with God and be expectant of His directions.

now

Stop seeking validation from others. Trust your discernment and God's voice.

Activation

Ask God if there is anyone you should be cautious about sharing information and revelation. Rest in what God has originally told you and don't waiver based on people's opinions. Repent if you feel like you have not sought God first and ask Him to give you peace in the middle of what you're facing.

Reflect

Do you find yourself oversharing information and revelation that God shares to you with others? If so, what do you overshare?

Why do you think you overshare information? Are you seeking validation/confirmation, just like to talk, etc.?

How can you strengthen hearing and knowing God's voice? How does He speak to you?

Pray

Father God, I ask that you help me to hear from you. Help me to not seek out validation from others in what you have spoken to me. Help me to trust what I hear from you and continue to be in communion with you. I repent for any oversharing and ask that you help me to learn to become quiet in the revelations you share with me. I ask that you remove ungodly voices and instructions from my spirit. I ask that you help me to tune out any voices that are not operating from your spirit. I ask that you replace it with your Holy Spirit and that I may be able to discern if the voice is from you or not. I thank you for giving me clarity and discernment in my heart, spirit, and dreams where you are leading me. I thank you that you are making the path straight in which direction I should take. In Jesus' mighty name, amen.

Day 1

Where is Your Accountability?

"Where there is no guidance the people fall, but in an abundance of counselors there is victory."

Proverbs 11:14, NASB

At the end of church service, I went to the altar to request prayer. I spoke with the same two people all the time. They prayed over me in many areas that I was concerned with and reminded me that God has my back. I didn't think that my interactions with them would be more than that. However, over time, I talked with them over the phone for hours. They are great encouragers. They held me accountable to God's Word and the calling He has on my life. They saw things I didn't always see and weren't afraid to keep it real with me. They pray for me and lead me to check with God to see what the Lord has to say.

Great accountability will always lead you back to God. They won't go out of God's Word and will uplift you. Seek godly counsel and be careful of who you speak to and who you allow to speak into your life. If who you are seeking counsel from doesn't lead you to God or hold you accountable to his Word, it's time to find some true godly counsel. They won't be timid in holding you to the Lord's standards, and you are to keep them accountable for what they say. As I reflect, I realize that there were times when I trusted in the wrong people for guidance. I often ended up feeling more confused, discouraged, doubtful, and sometimes fearful. When you have the right accountability, you won't walk away feeling negative emotions or feel further from God. Your accountability circle doesn't need to be a whole bunch of people. It's better to have a few people you trust and know won't gossip about you. Accountability is important because you will get more of an understanding of where you are and where you want to be. You will recognize the changes that you need to make. You will have a safety-net of people that can help you if you fall and your faith will grow stronger.

now

We are not meant to do life alone. Always seek
the Lord in whom you can trust.

Activation

Send a message of appreciation to your accountability partner(s). It can be a hand-written note, text message, email, etc. Share how thankful you are for them and how they have helped you along your journey.

Reflect

Who do you consider accountability partners for you, if at all?

____

____

____

____

What traits do these accountability partners share, and how are you left feeling afterwards?

____

____

____

____

What are some areas of your life they are holding you accountable for and what progress have you made so far?

____

____

____

____

Have you trusted in the wrong counsel? What changes have you made to stop this from recurring?

Pray

Father God, I pray that you surround me with the right people to uplift me and guide me. I pray for individuals to come into my life and speak the Word of God over me. I pray that you would flow through them and that I would be receptive to my mind and heart being renewed and transformed. Anyone that was not sent by you or is sowing discouragement and doubt, I ask that you remove them from my circle. God, I ask that you place people in my life that will hold me accountable to your Word. I pray that you guard my heart and mind against any spirit that is not of you that may come to steal, kill, and destroy the faith I have. Help me to tune out anything that is not of you and to be focused on hearing your voice. Give me the strength and courage to want to be transformed and to come into full alignment with your perfect will for my life. In Jesus' mighty name, amen.

Day 8

Purify My Heart

"Create in me a clean heart, O God, and renew a right spirit within me."

Psalm 51:10, ESV

God wants to purify us from anything that is not like Him. The purification process is not easy and often involves things being removed from us. Habits, mindsets, and strongholds must break for us to walk in full freedom. The definition of purify means: to cleanse, to refine, to redeem, and to be free. We often say to God, "Purify me and cleanse my heart," but are we willing to undergo the uncomfortable process of purification? When the Lord started speaking to me about being sexually pure, I honestly didn't think I could do it. The Lord was and still is very patient with me. A part of me wanted to be more like Christ and a part of me wanted to still glorify my flesh. A part of me wanted to start the journey of being sexually pure and free and a part of me didn't want to give up sex. Obedience is better than sacrifice (1 Samuel 15:22). The Lord was calling me higher, and I was afraid of what that was going to look like. I started that journey two years ago, and I'm still walking it out. God also wants our hearts to be cleansed and to be able to do His will.

Some of you are sexually abstinent but have an impure attitude. God sees that as well. “Blessed are the pure in heart, for they shall see God,” (Matthew 5:8, ESV). There were problems with my attitude with some people, and the Lord made me aware of it. He had to extract those things in me that were not of Him and replace it with Christ’s love. There are things that the Lord wants to extract and replace in us, and it may be a difficult process for some. Several things will be more challenging to change and let go. However, we may willingly let go of other things easier. We always want to make sure our heart is in the right place with God.

now

We may be able to fool others, but we can’t fool God.
He knows our heart.

Activation

Meditate on these Scriptures: Job 23:10 and Psalm 139:23.

Reflect

Ask the Lord what He wants to purify in you. List these things here.

Are you resistant or more accepting of the purification process? Ask the Lord how you can go through this process and come out better than before?

What changes will you have to make to be able to be purified and refined? What would this look like for you?

Pray

Father God, create in me a clean heart and renew the right spirit in me. Help me to remove any impurities and replace them with your heart desires. Help me to not shy away from the process of purification but embrace the transformation you desire in me. Give me strength in the process when I feel weak or don't know where to turn. Remind me of your promises and your faithfulness when I feel like I'm unable to move forward in being refined. Thank you for walking with me and calling me higher. Thank you for not giving up on me and being patient with me. Help me to see myself as you see me. I repent for anything that I have done that is not pure in your eyes. I thank you that the blood of Jesus washes me clean. I thank you for restoring me and giving peace even in the middle. In Jesus' mighty name, amen.

Day 9

Diamond in the Rough

"For it is God who works in you to will and to act in order to fulfill his good purpose."

Philippians 2:13, NIV

One morning, I woke up from a dream. I was at a formal party and that seemed to go on forever. I started to fall asleep on the couch and I saw someone coming over. I quickly stretched my legs out like I didn't see them coming. The dream ended. I remember asking the Lord what it was about. He illuminated to me a part of myself that I didn't realize. He told me that He is working out the selfish part of me. The Holy Spirit didn't hold back. I laughed with God because I could see what He was talking about when He showed me the dream. I was thinking about how tired I was and my needs. I wasn't thinking about sharing the couch with that person because I wanted to get a good rest.

There are rough qualities that are not so pretty, and God is working out in all of us before marriage. God knows our hearts. We may be able to fool man, but we can't fool God. Some of us have a bad attitude, are selfish, lazy about certain things, and have a walk-away attitude. God wants to correct aspects of ourselves before we enter marriage. If we don't fix these qualities, they will be magnified once we get married.

God still sees us as precious, despite these rough qualities we have. God knows we need some polishing and refinement, and He is the best one to do it! You may feel compressed on all sides, however, diamonds are created under intense pressure. Don't be afraid to let God polish you. When He does, you will sparkle more than you ever did before.

Now

You just may be a diamond in the rough!

Activation

Pray and ask God what rough qualities you portray. Please understand that there is no shame. None of us are perfect. We first must be transparent with God so that He may purify those things that are not of Him in us.

Reflect

What rough qualities did God mention?

____

____

____

____

Were you aware of these qualities? Were any of them a shock to you?

____

____

____

____

In what ways will God help you to correct those qualities?

____

____

____

____

Pray

Father God, thank you for seeing me as precious. Thank you for valuing me and calling me yours. Help me to see what needs to be transformed in me. Illuminate to me the areas I may have forgotten about or not aware of that should be changed. Father God, help me to realize that I'm not perfect, but I serve a perfect God. Help me to not be resistant to the changes that you want to do in me. Help me to see you as the potter and I'm clay. You are shaping me to your desires for my life. Smooth any areas that are rough in me. Purify my heart and my spirit to line up with the Word of God and the will that you have for me. Help me to continue this process with a good attitude, despite how I really feel. Give me a new vision to see me how you see me. Help me to change my perspective and remove anything that is not like you in me. In Jesus' mighty name, amen.

Day 10

God's Waiting Room

"Wait for the LORD; be strong and take heart and wait for the LORD."

Psalm 27:14, NIV

I have felt all kinds of emotions while in God's waiting room. I have felt frustrated, anxious, clingy, disappointed, and even apathetic. I have learned to be content in God's waiting room. We have all experienced moments of feeling like we are in God's waiting room. For some of us, we have been waiting so long that it may feel like our name will never be called. For some of us, we have become agitated or anxious in the waiting room. We may even start to doubt and wonder if our marriage promise will truly come to pass.

How we wait matters to God. He is seeing if we will be obedient and wait for what He has for us. Some of us may have felt like walking out of the waiting room because it's taking too long. Don't walk out on the promise because you never know when your name will be called. God has not forgotten about you, and His time is always right. Don't focus on the names that are being called before you. Some of you may have felt like you have been waiting first. Trust God to know that He is working behind the scenes, and it will all come together in his way and in his time.

now

Anything worth having is worth waiting for.
It will be worth the wait!

Activation

Meditate on the following Scriptures:

- Isaiah 64:4
- Colossians 1:11
- Psalm 130:5
- Romans 8:18
- Galatians 6:9
- Hebrews 11:1
- Psalm 46:10
- Psalm 37:7-9
- Jeremiah 29:11
- 2 Peter 3:8
- Mathew 6:33
- Psalm 31:24
- 1 Peter 5:10
- Romans 12:12
- 2 Peter 3:9
- James 5:11

- Lamentations 3:25
- Isaiah 40:31
- Psalm 33:20-22
- Proverbs 3:5-6
- Romans 5:3-4
- Psalm 62:5

Reflect

While in God's waiting room, what has been your experience regarding your marriage promise?

____

____

____

____

What has your attitude been like during the wait?

____

____

____

____

What changes are you willing to make to shift your attitude in God's waiting room?

____

____

____

____

Pray

Father God, I thank you for wanting your best for me. Thank you for not overlooking me and that I'm not forgotten by you. Thank you for preparing my mind, heart, soul, and spirit in this waiting process. Thank you for preparing and healing my future husband's heart, mind, and soul. Despite what I see, I will operate in faith and not fear. I will speak life and not death. I will choose to be obedient, even when my flesh wants to do what is contrary to your commands. Forgive me for going ahead of you and my lack of patience. I repent for any of my actions that were not in alignment. I ask that you help me to understand the wait and what you're doing. I ask that you give me clarity in anything that seems cloudy or that I don't understand. I ask you to help me to work on my current assignments while in the wait. I will focus on me. I will focus on my tasks and what you are expecting of me in this season. Thank you for choosing me and appointing me. Help me to work on my purpose each day. I know that you desire my obedience. Help me to wait well and with the right attitude. My faith is not contingent upon what I see in the natural, but I will speak the Word. Continue to cleanse me while in the wait and help me to fix my focus on the things of heaven. In Jesus' mighty name, amen.

Day 11

A Millimeter Away

"For nothing will be impossible with God."

Luke 1:37, ESV

One night, before heading upstairs to get ready for bed, I was watching the television and aimlessly shooting at the dart board. I didn't think I was going to get close to the bullseye. Half the time I ended up hitting the wall, not even close to making it on the board. Without really trying, I was one dot away from bullseye. In disbelief, I looked again at how close I was to landing on the bullseye. One dot away! I realized how close some of us are to a certain breakthrough in our lives. In this situation, I wasn't really trying. I wasn't putting in my best effort.

Sometimes, we can release and just let things happen the way God wants them to happen. We may be caught off-guard as to how close we are to the promise. For some of us, we are close to our promised kingdom marriage, and we don't realize it or see it.

now

Don't give up. You may just be a millimeter away.

Activation

Think about how many times you were close to something without even trying. Ask the Lord how close you are to your kingdom marriage.

Reflect

What is a time in your life when you were close to achieving something without trying? How did you respond? How did it make you feel?

How close are you to your kingdom marriage? If the Lord hasn't answered you, simply wait for his response. You may have to come back later to write this part.

What ways are you able to be more carefree and rest in God?

Pray

Father God, I thank you for observing my every step. I thank you for guiding me in the direction that you want me to go. Help me to truly rest and be carefree in you. Help me to fully surrender and release control to you. You know my thoughts before it comes into my mind. You know every step before I move. Help me to release the things that are weighing on my heart, mind, and spirit. I release my worries to you, and I leave them at your feet. In Jesus' mighty name, amen.

Day 12

Delight in Him

"Delight yourself in the LORD, and he will give you the desires of your heart."

Psalm 37:4, ESV

God reminded me of this Scripture many times. He wanted me to seek His face and delight in Him first and always. The Lord knows our heart's desires. As we delight in Him, He will give us what to want. Many of you already know that God has placed a strong desire in your heart for marriage; it is not there by accident. Don't feel like something is wrong about having this strong desire because it is a part of God's purpose for your life. We shouldn't idolize or put anything in front of God, but it's okay to have that desire. As we delight in Him, we find peace and joy. We find safety in knowing that God is a good, a good father and friend. God is not a God to trick you or play with your heart. If He has put the desire in your heart, trust in His will that it will come to pass.

We must make Him our focus, that He is good even if He doesn't, He is still good. God is more than enough for us. As we spend time with Him through prayer and worship, our bond will grow stronger. Intimacy with God is vital. He wants connection and to be number one in our life. We must remove anything or anyone that is steering us away from

God being number one in our lives. Enjoy being in God's presence and growing deeper into the things of the spirit.

now

Make God your number one—everything.

Activation

Spend a few minutes esteeming God. Talk about how much He means to you, how you need Him, how He has helped you, and how He has been a friend and a father. This will help to build intimacy with God.

Reflect

Have you been delighting yourself in God and in God alone? What does this look like for you?

____

____

____

____

Is there anything you are placing in front of God? Identify those people and things.

____

____

____

____

What is it that God is desiring of you in this season as you delight in Him?

____

____

____

____

Pray

Father God, I choose to delight in you for everything I desire. God, help me to make you my focus and to filter everything through you. I understand that Jesus, you're my promise. I thank you for giving me a marriage promise and that you will fulfill this desire in your time. Thank you for seeing my desires. Help me to align them with you. Thank you, God, for being everything and more that I could want or need. Thank you for reminding me that I'm worthy of love because you first loved me. There is no greater love than you Jesus, you satisfy my heart. You fill those empty places. Fill me with your overflowing peace and love. Thank you for being abba father, prince of peace, and the lover of my soul. Thank you for bestowing blessings that are out of this world. In Jesus' mighty name, amen.

Day 13

Let God In

"Here I am! I stand at the door and knock. If anyone hears my voice and opens the door, I will come in and eat with that person, and they with me."

Revelation 3:20, NIV

During some moments in my life, I hadn't let God into the places where healing was needed. God wanted to come and remove the hurt, trauma, and disappointment that was overwhelming me. I wanted to let God in my heart. He knew my heart more than anyone. Sometimes I projected my fears and insecurities onto God. I had a fear of God not being faithful to me, even though He has proved himself time and time again. I had a fear of being abandoned or left, but God still was with me. I had a fear of not being chosen or being enough in His eyes, yet He had chosen me before the foundation of this Earth. He calls me beloved, a masterpiece, and I'm His. I had a fear of not being loved, but He said, "I have loved you with an everlasting love."

I encourage you to open the door for Jesus, prepare a place for Him. Don't close off your heart to Him. He wants to be with you. God's very nature is not intrusive or forceful, He wants to be invited. Choosing to let God in, despite what others may have done. It's freeing. God knows how to comfort and approach us, even in the littlest of things. He speaks to us, sees us, and He wants to spend time with us.

now

God already knows our heart. We might as well let Him into our hearts.

Activation

Visualize where God is in your life, where you think He fully wants to be in your life and what it looks like.

Reflect

What places have you not fully given God access to in your life?

____

____

____

____

What has caused you to withhold certain areas of your life to God?

____

____

____

____

How do you think God perceives you? Has this affected the relationship you both have?

____

____

____

____

What would it look like to let God into your heart and space?

Pray

Father God, I let you into my heart. I let you into those dry places that seem empty. I thank you for always seeking me and not leaving me. I let you in because I know you are the only one who truly gets me. You have created me and call me yours. You have designed me just as you saw fit. You knew the secret battles I would face, the tears I would cry, and the heaviness that my heart would feel. I thank you for restoring me. I thank you for healing every broken and damaged place that's in me. I thank you for drawing close to me as I draw close to you. I prepare a place for you in my mind and in my heart. I prepare a place for your Holy Spirit to cover anything that is not of you. Father God, remove any fears I may have and replace it with your everlasting love. Remove any insecurities I have and replace it with your guidance and peace. Thank you, God, for delivering me. Thank you for being my heavenly Father. In Jesus' mighty name, amen.

Day 14

What Are You Building?

"Commit to the Lord whatever you do, and he will establish your plans."

Proverbs 16:3, NIV

In my season of singleness, I realized this is my time to build and to work on the goals and plans that I have for myself. My assignments are being a full-time graduate student, working part-time and full time, and building Janay Cosmetics and The Janay Wells Show. My assignments require work, time, and commitment! We have assignments from God in our singleness that require attention and focus. We must focus on what God is doing in us before we can focus on what God wants to do through us.

Be faithful in the season you're in, and God will enlarge your territory. In your season of singleness, you can spend your time and money however you want. When you're married, it won't always be about what you want, your plan, and your vision. You will then have joint purposes and destinies that you must work on together accomplish. You both will have to make sacrifices and compromises, that aren't necessarily easy. However, love is sacrificial. Jesus is the perfect example. Focus on your kingdom assignment before you will become preoccupied with your kingdom marriage assignments. When you focus on your assignment at hand, the other great tasks will come. You will be ready and prepared for the bigger assignments. “If you are faithful in little things, you will be faithful in large ones. But if you are dishonest in little things, you won’t be honest with greater responsibilities,” (Luke 16:10, NLT). When you are building, don’t compare what you are doing with others.

God has you in a season and purpose that may be different. Some people may be getting married before you and you may feel like the last one out. However, there is purpose and work to do while waiting. If you spend quality time during your season of waiting, you are building a strong foundation for your marriage to come. The enemy doesn’t want you to build. Have your stake in the ground and take it by force. Piece by piece, block by block, you are building, and it will all come together as one unit. Be faithful in your building season.

now

Keep building faithfully and watch how all your assignments connect for a greater purpose.

Activation

Do one thing today that will help you get closer to building your goal and vision.

Reflect

What are you working on in this season that God wants you to build for His kingdom?

____

How has your attitude been in this time of building?

What kind of impact or influence do you want to have in your kingdom assignments? What would that look like?

Pray

Father God, I thank you for the tasks you have given me now to complete before my kingdom marriage. I ask that you help me to focus on the projects and mission that you have for me now. I thank you for blessing the works of my hands and that everything that I touch shall prosper and succeed. I will continue to build what you have given me with the right attitude. Help me to not complain and to continue to have faith in what you're doing in me. I ask that you connect me with the right connections and places in my building season. I ask that you show me favor in what I'm building and that it will bring more glory to your kingdom. In Jesus' mighty name, amen.

Day 15

Fear Has to Bow

"I sought the Lord and he answered me; he delivered me from all my fears."

Psalm 34:4, NIV

One day as I was sitting, I thought, "It's on the way." I was excited, but fear came over me. Would I be a great wife? Would he be understanding and accommodating of some of my health issues? Would he leave when things get rough? Would he treasure me? I could write a long list of fears. These worrisome thoughts started to flood my mind. I questioned if I would be enough and if God was sure that I had this calling. Some of my concerns included how I would be perceived, could he be faithful, and how might everything fall into place.

I knew that God didn't just see me for where I'm today, but who and where I will be throughout the course of my life.

"God does not give us the spirit of fear, but of power, love, and a sound mind," (2 Timothy 1:7, NKJV). If you are having fearful thoughts and feelings, recognize that this is not of God. Fear is a lie and is used to get us to focus on just that. Fear is a distraction. Some of us have fears of not being found or insecurities of trusting our future husband's fidelity. Fear is false evidence appearing real. Most of the time what we are fearing, may not come true and is often distorted. We must fix our focus on God and what He is doing.

Now

Fear is a lie and is used to paralyze us
from moving forward.

Activation

Ask God what fears you have while in the waiting process. Ask God to help deliver you from those fears and to fill you with His perfect love.

Reflect

What present fears do you have in finding the man God has for you or maintaining a relationship with the man that God has for you?

What fears do you have regarding your future kingdom marriage?

What does fear look like for you (e.g., worry, physical manifestations, sleep issues, overthinking, etc.)? How can you reduce this fear?

Pray

Father God, I thank you that your perfect love is driving out each fear. I thank you that you are coming to overwhelm the things that are overwhelming me. I thank you God that you haven't given me a spirit of fear, but of love, power, and a sound mind. I ask that you restore my mind and continue to activate your peace that transcends all understanding. I ask that you speak to my heart about anything concerning me. I ask that you help me to heal any insecurities that are driving these fears. I thank you that in your presence, fear must bow, it must flee. I thank you that fear no longer has a hold of me. I can walk knowing that you are with me and that you lead me by still waters. In Jesus' mighty name, amen.

Day 16

Trust the Process

"Trust in the Lord with all your heart and lean not on your own understanding, in all your ways submit to him, and he will make your paths straight."

Proverbs 3:5 NIV

When I think of what the word *process* means, I don't think of it in a positive light. I believe that the *process* will take a long time, is perilous, anxiety-provoking, sacrificial, and painful. When I think of the process before the kingdom marriage, these same feelings are evoked. I wonder how long it is going to take. Will I be fully whole or ready? Will something that I thought was healed or delivered come back and rear its nasty head? Is he ready and whole? Will he be prepared to fully commit to just one person? Many fears and insecurities were brought up while processing my thoughts and emotions. I knew I had to seek the Lord to understand how to walk this process out.

We often don't want to go through the process to obtain something. Perhaps we may want a college degree, but not go through the tests, the papers, projects, etc. We may want to get a house, but not go through the process of saving money, not purchasing items we want to buy, and applying for the loan. We may want to buy a brand-new car, but not go through the process of what that requires. Many times, we want something that is achievable, but we don't want to make the necessary required sacrifices. We may desire to have a spouse but praying for one and preparing for one are two different things, which is a process. God is ordering steps and we must trust Him in this process. Many times, we may look and not see what God said in the natural.

We must continue to walk in faith and trust that God is working everything together behind the scenes. It may not be happening when we want it, but God knows where He is leading us. At times, it may feel like we are walking all alone, even though God never leaves us. It may seem at times that we are suffering and not sure why. We may start to wonder if we are on the right track or if we made a mistake. Oftentimes, when you embark on God's will for your life, it may seem like things are more difficult. Friendships and relationships may change, you may switch jobs, or move to a different location. We may not always see where God is taking us, but indeed, He is taking us to a place He has already prepared for us. We must lean not on our own understanding. We must acknowledge God. He is the one who knows. He knows more than everyone else we run to; He has it already set up. The Scripture says, "He will make our path straight." So, trust in the Lord, despite what you don't see. Trust that God has you and He is directing your paths.

Now

You either trust God or you don't.

Activation

Take a walk with God and see where He leads you. Listen to His voice. Be still enough to hear what He wants to speak to you.

Reflect

What did God speak to you as you were walking with Him?

What are you learning as you are going through this process? How would you rate your trust level with God on a scale of one to 10 (10 being the highest level of trust)? Be honest with yourself and with God.

How can you increase your level of trust in Him?

Pray

Father God, thank you for helping me in this process as I'm preparing for the kingdom marriage you have for me. Help me to let go of the things that you want me to let go. Help me to embrace the new things you have for me. Give me strength in the journey and hope to continue to grow even when I don't understand. Thank you for making my paths straight. I will trust in you and not lean on my own understanding. I will acknowledge you in all areas of my life and try not to jump ahead of you. Thank you for trusting in me and equipping me. Thank you for never leaving me. Thank you for being faithful even when I have been faithless. I will keep trusting in you. I will fix my eyes on you and the kingdom of heaven. I know that at the right place and time, it will happen. In Jesus' mighty name, amen.

Day 11

See-nothing Seasons

"For we walk by faith, not by sight."

2 Corinthians 5:7, ESV

The Lord had been speaking to me, and it seemed like nothing was taking place. Sometimes it felt like the very opposite, regression instead of progression. Sometimes I wondered why the Lord shared prophetic dreams and visions with me. It didn't make sense! It still doesn't make sense! The Lord may show you glimpses and even speak to you in different ways. First, you're not weird, and when you start to see those things come to pass, don't find it strange. Sometimes the Lord will spiritually reveal people, places, and events to you before you walk into it naturally. It will come to you full circle. It will start to make sense as God's will starts to unfold in your life.

So, when you feel like you're entering a due season, but you don't see any manifestations, press forward. God is working in your waiting, so keep moving forward. It can feel like we are standing, even battling between a prayer and a promise from God. Some of you have been praying and fasting, and still feel like nothing is moving. When you know you have a marriage promise, hang on to it, despite what it looks like. God hears your prayers, and He has not forgotten about you. You are not overlooked. Trust what God is doing in this time, even when you don't understand it.

now

When you see nothing, God sees everything.

Activation

Ask God to show you in the spirit where you are. Ask Him to continue to reveal His wonder. Continue to listen to Him as He speaks to you. Start to journal your encounters with God in relation to this promise. When you see certain things come to pass, go back, and put the date when it came to pass next to the specific encounter you had with Him.

Reflect

Do you feel like you are in a see-nothing season? If so, how are you responding to it?

____

____

____

____

What keeps your faith alive when you feel like you are in a see-nothing season?

____

____

____

____

What Scriptures help you during this time? If you don't know any, search Scriptures that are related to walking by faith.

____

____

____

____

Pray

Father God, I thank you that you are working despite what I see. Help me to walk by faith and not by sight. Help me to not look at the natural circumstances that are taking place. Help me to focus on the words you have spoken to me. Help me to not speak out of my unbelief or insecurities, but to continue to speak the words you have given me. Help me to be focused, here and now. I thank you God that when it seems like nothing is happening, you are orchestrating many things behind the scenes; things that will bring joy and blessings into my life. I thank you for walking with me and carrying me through every season. I thank God that I'm weathering the wait and I won't give up despite what I see. I thank you God for testing my faith and strengthening me in the wait. Thank you for letting me see how all this will work together later. What I may not be able to see or understand now, it will all make sense later. Thank you for protecting me during see-nothing seasons. I ask that you guard my heart, soul, spirit, and mind as I continue to wait for the proper time and season. In Jesus' mighty name, amen.

Day 18

Quit Stealing the Pen

"Be still and know that I am God."
Psalm 46:10, NIV

I've surrendered control and worry, then go back to doing so. I truly wanted God to write my love story, but I had an internal battle—not fully surrendering control. When I say this quote: "God is writing your story, quit trying to steal the pen. Trust the author," (unknown), I was instantly reminded about my struggle of how I stole the pen. I repented, gave it back to God, then stole the pen again. Some people struggle with this more than others.

If you are a planner, Type A personality, and typically like to know the details, you may struggle with letting go of full control. This can be rooted in fear, pride, and a lack of trust in God. If anybody can do it, God can! Sometimes we think we know better, or we try to manipulate situations, whether we mean to or not. This can further delay what God is trying to do behind the scenes. We must get out of God's way if we want Him to get the glory in our story. God doesn't need our help! He is God and He is God all by himself. Sometimes we can get ahead of God by moving too quickly or wanting to know the master plan. Be still and surrender the things you are wondering about and trying to figure out. Rest in the goodness of who He is and what He already knows. In Psalm 23, it says: "He leads me by still waters and green pastures." Sometimes God will allow you to be tired out from worry and anxiety so that you can learn to truly rest in Him.

Now

God can do it way better than we can.
Trust in his divine plan and time.

Activation

Put on a worship song about surrendering. Speak in your heavenly language if you can. When you do this, you are praying God's will and the enemy can't understand you. Release any concerns or worries you have been feeling. Rest in who God is and what He knows. Rest in Him.

Reflect

Are you trying to steal the pen? If so, what areas are you not fully surrendering to the Lord?

What do you think could be causing you to not fully trust God with your promised kingdom marriage?

What are some ways you can let go and fully yield to the Lord? What would this look like for you?

What are some ways that you can rest in God's presence?

____

____

____

____

Pray

Father God, thank you for the great plans you have for me. Help me to rest in the process of the wait. You're the God of the middle. Help me to rest in what you have already declared. I fully surrender my plans and will to you. I repent for when I let worry or doubt consume me. You are writing my love story and if I want you to get the glory, I must move out of your way. Help me to learn to trust in your plan even when I don't understand. Help me to realize that your ways and thoughts are higher. Help me to stop stealing the pen and wanting to take over. Help me to release all control over my marriage promise. Help me to fully rest in the wait. Help me to not be focused on the details of the who, what, when, where, and how. Help me to surrender my thoughts and worries to you. I come boldly into your throne room and acknowledge that you are God, and you are God alone. It is my role to trust and be obedient in what you ask of me. Help me to not shy away out of fear or doubt, but to continue to pray and intercede for my future spouse. In Jesus' mighty name, amen.

Day 19

Signed. Sealed. Delivered!

"No good thing does the Lord withhold from those who walk uprightly."

Psalm 84:11, ESV

"Signed, Sealed, Delivered" by Stevie Wonder was played over the speaker while I was in the dressing room at work. My coworker and I danced to the beat and were being silly. God's promises are already signed, sealed, and awaiting an appointed time to be delivered. Jeremiah 29:11 says. "He knows the plans that He has for you." Sometimes we may wonder when it will be His timing for our kingdom marriage promise. For some, years have passed, and you may start to question if the Lord wants you to be married. Don't give up hope! We must put faith in God that He is tracking the promises He has for us. It's coming and it's here now.

Whenever I order something online, I get super excited when I know that it has been shipped and on its way to me. I get more excited when I see that it arrived. God does not want us to lose our hope and our joy when it comes to His plans for our lives. Unlike a package ordered online, we can't track God's heavenly packages to us. It may come as a surprise. He may hint to you that it is on the way. However, our package hasn't been lost or delivered to someone else, it's still coming. His promises for us are sealed in heaven and He knows the right time to deliver. To this day, when I hear the song, I think about how God will deliver His plans and promises on time. We must put our trust and hope in Jesus, who is our heavenly promise awaiting to return as well.

Now

Trust God's perfect timing. He will deliver on time!
Let us wait expectantly for God's promises.

Activation

Ask God what the status is of some of the blessings. Are they here, on the way, coming much later?

Reflect

What are some of the things the Lord has told you about your marriage promise?

____

____

____

____

After weathering in the wait, will you still have the expectation that God will deliver your marriage promise to you? What are some things that have lessened your expectation and joy?

____

____

____

____

What are some ways you can increase your faith in your marriage promise that you haven't seen manifest?

____

____

____

____

Pray

Father God, I thank you that my future kingdom marriage is signed and sealed by you. I thank you God that no promise you have for me will be withheld, that your word shall go forth and accomplish what it has been sent for to accomplish. I thank you that none of your words shall return to you void. I thank you for removing any hindrances and delays. I thank you that in your perfect timing, my marriage blessing will be delivered just in time. I thank you that I don't have to worry about the status and tracking of my blessings. I thank you that you watch over your word to perform it. I ask that you remove any fear, doubt, and worry that I have over the timing of my marriage blessing. I thank you for keeping me in peace and faith. I thank you God that my faith is activating spiritual keys in heaven and that you are always moving behind the scenes. You never sleep or slumber and I thank you for moving on my behalf. Help me to not become anxious in the wait, but to patiently wait on you during this time of wonder. In Jesus' mighty name, amen.

Day 20

I Said What I Said

"So take courage! For I believe God. It will be
Just as He said."

Acts 27:25, NLT

Many times, the enemy confronted me, challenging what God spoke to me.
I was wrestling with this one day and God spoke to me and said, "You either believe what I have said, or you believe the enemy."

"Okay," I thought.

God was pretty much saying to me, "I have answered you and my say is final."

The enemy's challenges are not anything new. The enemy has been doing that since the Garden of Eden with Adam and Eve. He challenges what God has already spoken to sow seeds of doubt. In the Garden of Eden, the woman said to the serpent, "We may eat fruit from the trees in the garden, but God did say, 'You must not eat fruit from the tree that is in the middle of the garden, and you must not touch it, or you will die. You will not certainly die," the serpent said to the woman. "For God knows that when you eat from it your eyes will be opened, and you will be like God, knowing good and evil," (Genesis 3:2-4, NIV). The enemy wants to come and twist what God had spoken to you. He wants to make us question what God said. We must stand firm on what God has shown and spoken to us. The enemy always tries to go against God's order and instruction.

The root of this is pride. Many of us have things that the Lord has shown and confirmed to us multiple times. Many have faced doubt and confusion, thinking a situation or person can't be from the Lord. The enemy is trying to use your confusion to cause you to step out of the place of faith when it doesn't exactly look like how God said. The person may not be acting like what God showed you.

Despite the enemy's tactics, God didn't disqualify you from knowing about the blessing. God knew you were going to doubt or overstep at times. We repent and get back in alignment with God. He knew, but despite this, He still chose to trust you. Many times, the warfare and opposition come when God has revealed certain pieces of information and the enemy is threatened. The enemy continuously denounces and opposes kingdom marriages, unity, and obedience to the Lord. However, despite what it looks like, we must stand firm on His Word and promises.

now

God has the final say and that's it.

Activation

Ask God how you are equipped to stand firm on His Word. Ask him how your faith and confidence can increase in Him.

Reflect

What has God spoken to you regarding your kingdom marriage promise?

____

____

____

____

How has the enemy tried to challenge you in what God has spoken?

____

____

____

____

What ways has God told you to stand firm on his word? What Scriptures are in your arsenal to fight back against the enemy's schemes?

____

____

____

____

Pray

Father God, I thank you for speaking to me. I thank you for keeping me informed of your Word. I thank you that each word shall go forth and do what it was sent to accomplish. I thank you that none of your words shall return onto you empty. I ask that you quiet the mouth of the enemy right now. I ask that each seed of doubt and confusion that has been planted by the enemy, fails, and is uprooted. I thank you for every dream, vision, and Scripture you have given me. I thank you for revealing to me what you want to speak to me and show me in this moment. I thank you that it may not look 100% what you have shown me right now. I thank you that in due season, the Word will become flesh. I ask that you increase my faith in this season to believe what you have said. I thank you that you are a supernatural God who is more than capable of finishing what was started in me. I thank you that it will be just as you said. In Jesus' mighty name, amen.

Day 21

Nothing Wasted

"And we know that all things God works for the good of those who love him, who have been called according to His purpose."

Romans, 8:28, NIV

As I reflect on my life and think about the relationships that didn't work out, I consider how God will truly work all things together for our good. Sometimes we may feel that we have wasted time, energy, effort, and more. However, God hasn't lost count of everything we have done. He sees our heart and knows what we have sown. Nothing is wasted when it comes to God. He can find a purpose for our disappointments and hurts. He takes what other people meant for our harm and turns it around for our good. We may not know how God will work everything out, but trust that He will. Trust that he knows what's best for you. Trust that God is sovereign and His plans for you are greater than the ones you have for yourself.

Stop looking back, you aren't going that way. You are moving forward into the greatness the Lord has prepared for you. Trust that whoever left you, God accounted for that lost relationship. Trust that the missed opportunity has been accounted. Nothing catches God by surprise. He knew the people that would walk out of your life. Trust that God knows what's best for you, even when you can't see it right now. He is working all things out for your good!

now

God knows how to take everything, even the ugly stuff, and make it beautiful.

Activation

Look back in your life and start to praise God for His protection. Start to thank God for all the times you didn't think you could get back up and He gave you the strength to rise. Thank God that what the enemy tried to do didn't break you. Take a moment and give God all praise, glory, and honor.

Reflect

What have you been rescued from by God? Did He turn around heartbreaks and disappointments?

How did God work to turn around disappointments, failed relationships, and more for your good?

What surprised you the most from how God restored or gave recompense for what was lost?

Pray

Father God, I thank you that nothing has gone to waste. I thank you for replenishing everything that is missing or has been lost. I thank you that you are giving me recompense for everything that was stolen from me. I thank you that the setback, heartbreak, and disappointment didn't break me. I thank you for making beauty out of ashes. I thank you that you are the author of my story. You are the author and the finisher of my faith. I thank you for protecting me from harm seen and unseen. I thank you that I'm already victorious through Jesus Christ. Continue to guide my footsteps and help me hear your Holy Spirit even clearer. Give me wisdom and understanding in situations that I don't get. Give me peace to walk away from anything that is not of you or from you. Help me to change my perspective on some life events. Help me to understand that you are making this beautiful. I thank you God for walking with me and always being faithful. I thank you for redirecting my paths. In Jesus' mighty name, amen.

Day 22

Secrets from the Father's Heart

"Call to me and I will answer you and tell you great and unsearchable things you do not know."

Jeremiah 33:3, NIV

As I started to seek God more, He started revealing things to me. I knew that there are many mysteries to God, and I drew closer. I started to journal more and more and reflected (selah) at the end. Selah means to pause and reflect. Then I wrote what God was speaking to me. Sometimes we go to God, but we don't always give Him a chance to fully express what He would like to say back to us. God wants us to go to Him and He wants to be number one in our lives. What I have often found in my life and in the lives of others is sometimes we don't go directly to God. We may go to our best friend, our mother, and other people, but we forget to ask the one first who is all knowing.

God has "great and unsearchable things," but we must seek Him to find it. The Scripture says, "Call to me and I will answer you." God may not answer us when we want Him to, but He knows the right timing to reveal certain things. When we lean into God and seek His face, He reveals His heart to us. When we are after God's heart, we delight in Him and find joy and peace. We find rest for our souls because we know that God cares for us, and He wants to be near to us. He wants to reveal things to our heart and surprise us! The Lord wants to be good to us and He wants to reveal His glory and purpose in our lives. God is a good, good father and He has special things in store for us, but we must seek Him.

now

Heaven's hotline is 24/7, it's just one call away.

Activation

Ask God what are some of the secrets He may want to reveal to you from His heart.

Reflect

What or who have you been seeking after instead of God being your number one?

___

___

___

___

What are some of the secrets that God revealed to you during the activation?

___

___

___

___

Are you comfortable hearing God's voice for yourself? In what ways can you improve your communication with God?

___

___

___

___

Pray

Father God, I thank you for speaking with me and revealing your heart to me. I understand that I must seek you and call on you. I want you to be my number one priority. I repent for all the times I have not gone to you first and sought what man had to say. I understand that you have the final say and that your Word shall not return onto you void or empty. Father God, I thank you for sharing your heart with me. I thank you for being available to call and I know that you will always answer me. In Jesus' mighty name, amen.

Day 23

Stay the Course

"In their hearts humans plan their course, but the Lord establishes their steps."

Proverbs 16:9, NIV

We often believe our marriage promise will go the way we think. However, God knows what needs to take place and where we are. I have sometimes gotten frustrated in the process and wanted to take the next exit off the course. When it comes to your marriage promise, sometimes you may want to give up because of experiencing speed bumps and detours and felt delayed. God is rerouting and protecting you from harm, seen and unseen. You might have thought, "If I had taken that exit a long time ago, maybe I would be in a different place." You are right where you need to be. I know it sometimes feels like we may be behind or that people are passing us by. However, be reminded that the Lord is establishing your steps. He is making sure you're at the right places at the right time.

It is important to stay on the course the Lord has for us. When we try to rush ahead, it can cause more delays. Don't look behind and beside you. Don't become distracted on about location, but rather be content in where God has you now. You may become weary, wondering if you're going the right direction. Trust God's GPS (God Positioning System). He is tracking your every move and helping you get there in His way and time. Delay does not mean denial. Stay positioned, stay obedient, and stay the course. God will give you grace to finish the race.

Now

Your current location is not your final destination.

Activation

Ask God what He is doing in your life while you are staying the course He has for you.

Reflect

Where do you feel your location is on the course that God has for you?

____

____

____

____

What has your attitude been in response to delays, speedbumps, and detours?

____

____

____

____

If God were to give you the spouse right now, would you be ready for him?

____

____

____

____

What are some areas that God is trying to change in you as you are staying the course? Is there anything that you have allowed to pollute the atmosphere or temple that God has given you?

____

____

____

____

Pray

Father God, I thank you for giving me a finisher's anointing. What you have started in me, you will be faithful to complete. I thank you God that I'm not giving up on the promise, despite the course that I'm on now. Despite the hurdles and obstacles and detours that I have faced, I will continue to run and not grow weary. Despite what I have seen or have been feeling, I'm a winner through Christ. I thank you Jesus that you're my prize. I thank you God for choosing me and walking with me no matter where I run. You will never leave me or forsake me. I thank you God for pushing me to get back into the race when I want to give up. I thank you God for giving me grace to finish the race and finish strong. I thank you God for going ahead of me in this course and making a way for me. I thank you that I'm on the path and that I continue to pray for the path of my future husband. Wherever his path is, I know you are leading us towards each other. Our paths will cross, and our purposes will align. I thank you for leading and walking with us, despite the qualities that may make us feel that we are disqualified to run this race. I thank you for strengthening us so that we can eventually walk together as one. In Jesus' mighty name, amen.

Day 24

The Promise Still Stands

"Let us hold fast the confession of our hope without wavering, for he who promised is faithful."

Hebrews 10:23. ESV

One day, I just happened to click on one of Dr. Rhonda Mayes videos and I heard her say the Scripture above. I had not heard it before, and it resonated with me. At the time, I was wavering in the faith of my marriage promise, going from doubt to faith, back to doubt then back to faith. I knew what God told me about my marriage promise, so I asked why I often wavered. Sometimes, we can waiver in our faith in God for a certain promise by what we are seeing in the natural. For example, God told you that you would be getting married soon, but you don't see any potential candidates. Some of you know who your spouse is, but they aren't paying attention to you or may even be in a relationship with someone else. You may wonder, "Okay God, why did you even show me this?" Just know that God trusts you when He reveals information to you, even if it doesn't make full sense to you. Trust that God will put the pieces of the puzzle together. Sometimes He will show us a few pieces of the puzzle. Some of you may know the person, timelines, or other details. Some of you may not, and it's okay too. God is faithful in His promises to us, even when we are not faithful. Although, God knew we would go through the tests of our faith regarding our marriage promise. He still chose to trust us enough with the details. How awesome is this? Despite our wavering and disbelief, God still qualified us in His eyes to be able to pray and intercede regarding what He has shown us. We must hold fast and hold on to our hope, because the devourer comes to steal, kill, and destroy everything that is God's purpose in our life. Trust that your marriage promise will come to pass, but in His time.

now

Trust God, He knows what He is doing.
Choose to believe He is faithful.

Activation

Meditate on Hebrews 10:23 above and these Scriptures:

- Jeremiah 29:11
- 2 Corinthians 9:8
- Matthew 11:28-30
- John 10:10
- James 1:5

- Mark 11:24
- Psalm 37:4
- 2 Samuel 7:28
- James 1:17
- Psalm 100:5
- Psalm 84:11
- Isaiah 40:29
- Isaiah 43:2
- Philippians 4:6-7
- Proverbs 3:5

Reflect

Have you found yourself wavering in what God has told you about your marriage promise? If so, why? If you're not sure why, ask the Holy Spirit.

Ask the Lord if there have been any other influences that have caused you to waiver in your hope for your marriage promise?

What Scriptures help you to stay grounded in the Word of God and what He has told you?

Pray

Father God, thank you for being a promise-keeping God. Thank you that my kingdom marriage promise still stands. I ask that you help me to increase my faith and trust in you. Help me to have full confidence in you. I will hold fast to the confession of my faith without wavering. I repent for any wavering or mistrust I have had in you. Thank you for trusting me with what you have given. I understand that much is given, much is required. I thank you for believing in me and seeing me for not just who I'm now, but who I have already become. I will continue to walk by faith and not by sight. I will continue to seek your face and move as you instruct me. In Jesus' mighty name, amen.

Day 25

The Greater the Opposition. The Greater the Victory

"You will not have to fight this battle. Take up your positions; stand firm and see the deliverance the Lord will give you, Judah and Jerusalem. Do not be afraid; do not be discouraged. Go out to face them tomorrow, and the Lord will be with you."

2 Chronicles 20:17, NIV

When the Lord started to download more things into me regarding my kingdom marriage coming, I started to face a tremendous amount of warfare! I faced spiritual attacks in my dream, I struggled with doubt and anxiety, and my flesh got more in the way. I was so focused on what was happening and why, I lost my focus on what God was teaching me. It seemed like an uphill battle. The more I prayed for my future spouse, the more I tried to remain pure in my sexuality, and the more I was obedient to God. Sometimes I felt like I was doing something wrong. I was facing so much opposition. It was because I was following the Lord. I didn't understand. I still don't understand it fully, but the battle is not mine. The battle is the Lord's!

The enemy is threatened by us. When we decide to follow the Lord's will, we face opposition. We often want to give up on the promise because of a lack of understanding and not becoming weary due to warring in the spirit. God is strengthening us during this time. It can be hard to look at it this way, but He is making us stronger. He knows what the enemy is doing. He is allowing it to an extent because He knows it eventually will do a good work in us.

We have authority over the enemy's tactics. We can speak in our kingdom authority and the enemy must flee. We are already victorious through Jesus, and the battle is already won. Another Scripture says, "For He who is in you is greater than he who is in the world," (I John 4:4, ESV). When you feel weary in the wait because of the attacks, stand firm on the Word of God; the sword of the spirit. The enemy's lies and schemes. God will expose and will teach you how to take authority. We must understand that the enemy doesn't want unity and he doesn't want kingdom marriages to happen on the Earth. The enemy is jealous of the covenant we have with God and His love for us. Expect warfare and opposition to happen, but don't get overwhelmed. You're a threat, and the enemy knows it. When you're with God, you're already on the winning side!

now

You're being strengthened through this process. Don't focus on the attacks of the enemy. Focus on the God who has already defeated the enemy.

Activation

Ask the Lord how He is strengthening you in this season. Ask Him how to take full authority against the tactics of the enemy.

Reflect

What areas has the enemy been attacking you the most?

How does God want you to be strengthened during this process? What is He teaching you in this season?

What are some ways that are helping you to not fall for enemy schemes?

Pray

Father God, I thank you that you have equipped me with the sword of the spirit which is the Word of God. I thank you that I will stand firm and see the deliverance of the Lord. I thank you that no weapon formed against me shall prosper. I thank you that I don't need to fight this battle but take up my position and my authority in Jesus Christ. I thank you for being the strong tower that the righteous run to and are safe. I thank you for the helmet of salvation and the shield of faith. I put on the whole armor of God. Father God, teach me how to stand in my kingdom authority and speak your Word. I thank you for protecting me and guarding me against the schemes of the enemy. I thank you for being my fortress and a present help in times of trouble. I thank you that greater is he that is in me, than he that is in the word. I submit to God and resist the devil, and he shall flee. I thank you that I'm already victorious through Jesus Christ. In Jesus' mighty name, amen.

Day 26

Renewed Strength

"But those who wait for the Lord shall renew their strength; they shall mount up with wings like eagles; they shall run and not be weary; they shall walk and not faint."

Isaiah 40:31, ESV

There were times when I needed the Lord to renew my strength. Sometimes I felt weary in the journey because of the previous cycles I had been through. I was tired of being in short-term relationships that didn't last. I was tired of being attracted to men that weren't attracted to me or didn't want to commit. I was trying my best to live a holy and pure life, but it seemed to get more and more difficult. I wanted to follow God's will for my life, and as I continued, I felt like I was losing my strength. I was growing stronger and stronger, but it didn't feel like it.

We may grow weary and tired in the wait. We may feel like we have been waiting and waiting and want to stop believing altogether. However, those that wait upon the Lord shall renew their strength. The Lord doesn't necessarily tell us how long we may have to wait, but He does tell us that our strength would be renewed. You shall continue to run in the things of the Lord and not grow weary. You shall continue to walk into the new things that God has for you and not become faint. Stand firm on the Word of God and know that He has you. When you are weak, He is strong. When you're not sure, He is the answer.

Nugget of Wisdom

God is renewing your strength at times when you don't even know it. He will sustain you.

Activation

Have a conversation with God and ask Him why you have been wearied in the wait. Talk to Him about how you feel about this journey. Listen to "Wait on You" by Elevation Worship. It's on internet video websites. Worship while you wait!

Reflect

What areas do you feel weary regarding your kingdom marriage?

Is there anything that is making the weariness worse? Is there anything else that you're struggling with during this time?

What is God saying to you now in the process? How is He showing himself strong to you in this season when you feel weary?

Pray

Father God, thank you for giving me renewed strength. Thank you for being strong when I feel weak. Help me to not focus on how much farther I must go and have a heart of gratitude for how far you have allowed me to come. Help me to fix my focus on the things above, and not on Earthly things. Help me to realize that you walk with me, and when I can't walk, you carry me. Help me to see that this is a part of my preparation. Help me continue my race and continue without murmuring and complaining. Help me to understand that you are strengthening me, even though hurdles and obstacles are in my way. Thank you for working on my behalf. I may not understand everything now but thank you for giving me clarity in this season. Thank you for fixing my focus and allowing me to endure this process as you see fit. In Jesus' mighty name, amen.

Day 21

Tears of Joy

"Those who sow with tears will reap with songs of joy."

Psalm 126:5, NIV

God kept speaking to me...tears of joy, tears of joy, over and over in a particular season. One night I had a dream. I was at my favorite place to get dessert. Sometimes my friends tried to take me there when I felt sad or down because they knew it would cheer me up. There were so many flavor options, which in being awake, I often have a hard time choosing because I like them all. I then saw in the background a famous theme park, which was on my mind. I wanted to visit again because of the joy I experienced. Then, in the next scene, I was in an engagement proposal. He got down on one knee, and I cried. I mean the ugly cry. I couldn't stop. It was like every tear I cried regarding the promise was bursting out of my eyes, and I couldn't stop. I hope I don't look like that when the man God has for me proposes.

Be encouraged. God see your tears. He has them stored. This is how much He cares. He promises that He will turn your mourning into dancing and give you tears of joy. If you have been crying a lot, just know God is going to immeasurably restore your joy. If you have cried while wondering if God sees you, if He has forgotten about you, if you will ever get to the place of the vision He has put into your heart and mind, know that He does and He will! At times in my life, I cried so much that I needed an umbrella to deflect my tears. However, the sun does come up and He is giving you fresh joy!

now

God wants it more than you. Hang tight and watch Him move! Every heartbreak and disappointment are leading you to a greater outcome of joy.

Activation

Pray and be honest with God about how you have been feeling lately. Share with Him what you desire of Him and listen to hear what He desires for you in this season. Put on some music, dance, or just worship God. Give him thanks for what He is doing. Worship and thanksgiving must be your posture, despite what you don't see in your current season.

Reflect

Assess your emotions. Are you feeling sad, disappointed, joyful, or optimistic? Why?

____

____

____

____

Do you believe that God will turn around a situation for you? What or how do you think that would look?

____

____

____

____

What are some things you look forward to when meeting this person? If you have met this person, what do you look forward to in the future?

____

____

____

____

Pray

Father God, I thank you for bottling my tears. I thank you for seeing my sorrows and drawing close to me. Thank you that every tear of sadness, loneliness, and disappointment has been accounted for, and that you are a restorer. Thank you for the tears of joy that will be coming. Thank you for the blessings I can't see that will bring me joy and happiness. Thank you for being my comfort in seasons when I feel not seen or valued. Thank you for reassuring me that this too shall pass. Despair won't be my portion. Weeping may endure for a night, but joy is coming in the morning. I thank you God for restoring my peace and my joy. I thank you that I will be able to look back one day and see how you brought me out. I will be able to appreciate the blessings because I knew what it was like to feel the opposite. Father God, help me to treasure the moments I have with you. Remind me to step into your presence where there is fullness of joy. Thank you for seeing me and for loving me right where I am. Thank you for blessing me now and for working everything together for my good. In Jesus' mighty name, amen.

Day 28

Labor Pains

"When a woman is giving birth, she has sorrow because her hour has come, but when she has delivered the baby, she no longer remembers the anguish, for joy that a human being has been born into the world."

John 16:21, ESV

As you are approaching your kingdom marriage, you will most likely experience labor pains. Things will become more intense as time goes on and you may feel an urge to push. We may not want to wait as long as God intends. We may want to hurry the process along. However, a pregnant woman must wait nine months until she is able to see her baby. She feels the kicks, morning sickness, and other uncomfortable feelings. She is excited to welcome her new baby and sometimes may try to do things to get the baby out early. Have you ever heard of stories of women trying to accelerate the labor process? They may do activities such as walking, jumping on a trampoline, eating, and drinking certain foods and beverages, and more. We sometimes do things to help God out or accelerate the process.

Just like a pregnant woman, we must go through the uncomfortable process. Sometimes, a pregnant woman must push and other times she must relax. If she pushes too soon, she can cause harm to herself or the baby. When a woman is crowning, this is when you can see the baby's head in the birth canal. Some of us can see the Lord's promises over our lives as if it is getting ready to be birthed in our lives. Many of you are in the crowning, labor, or birthing season. When a woman is crowning, the feeling is often described as the "ring of fire". She normally feels a burning sensation and has the urge to push, and this is not the time to push. If she pushes during this stage, she can cause harm. We must learn when to push and the times to relax. We don't want to hinder or harm what God is trying to do in our lives. Some of you may feel the labor pains of your kingdom marriage coming. You may feel like you want to push but listen to God on when to push and when to relax. You don't want to prematurely give birth because this can come with more complications.

now

Labor is painful, but the promise is sweet.

Activation

Examine what the Lord has been testing you about. Examine the process of the promise and what feelings and experiences it has brought up in you. If you haven't experienced this part, it is okay. Some people will experience it differently. Just like natural pregnancy, some women have a rough experience while others have a smooth one.

Reflect

What has the Lord been contracting in your life that feels like labor pains?

____

____

____

____

What feelings have you been experiencing during the labor/birthing promise of your kingdom marriage, if any?

____

____

____

____

How has the Lord been easing the labor process for you, if any?

____

____

____

____

Pray

Father God, I thank you for the labor and delivery of this promise. I thank you that you are helping to ease the labor pains and other uncomfortable feelings that are starting to arise. I thank you that this promise is coming forth and it shall not delay. I thank you that you are doing a new thing and that comes with new experiences. Thank you for guiding me and loving me through this process. I thank you that it awaits an appointed time. I ask that you remove all barriers and hindrances that are trying to meet the labor process. I pray that you strengthen me when I feel weak and that you remind me of your Word. Help me to know when to push and when to relax. Help me to breathe through the process, no matter how uncomfortable it is. Thank you for guarding me and protecting me during this time. In Jesus' mighty name, amen.

Day 29

The Suddenlies of God

"Yes indeed, it won't be long now." God's Decree. Things are going to happen so fast your head will swim, one thing fast on the heels of the other. You won't be able to keep up. Everything will be happening at once- and everywhere you look, blessings! Blessings like wine pouring off the mountains and hills..."

Amos 9:13, MSG

During a conversation with God concerning my kingdom marriage, He said, "It will happen suddenly."

Because of my obedience, I have entered a season of acceleration. For some of you, God has told you it would swiftly happen for you. You may not be in a three-year, five-year, or even one-year relationship of dating or courting. It may happen sooner than this. We must get out of our own mind about when and how we want it to happen. God does not operate like we do. He has better plans than us. While growing up, I thought I would meet someone in college and date them for years before I got married. Well, I have graduated with my bachelor's degree, and it didn't happen. I'm working on my master's degree, and I'm not yet in a committed relationship. I'm okay with this. We can have our own ideal plans and times that aren't in accordance with God's plan. For some of you, it will be that sudden! The suddenlies of God can surprise us because we may not believe that it's happening before our very eyes. God wants to surprise us, and He wants to do it his way. Continue to be focused on what the Lord has for you to do, and before you know it, the manifestation of your marriage promise will be here.

now

Watch out, it may just suddenly happen!

Activation

Have a conversation with God about how you have been feeling in the wait. You may hear God download hints or glimpses to you. Pray in your heavenly language if you can. When you do this, you are praying to the will of God over your life and edifying yourself. The enemy can't understand you when you pray in the spirit.

Reflect

What expectations have you had of God regarding your marriage promise?

How have your expectations changed as you are becoming more aligned with God?

Are you receptive to God suddenly doing it His way? How does this make you feel? What fears do you have, if any?

Pray

Father God, thank you that you are the God of suddenlies. I thank you that you are preparing each step. I thank you for processing me and preparing me. I thank you that you can do it just like that! Give me the hope to continue believing in the promises you have for me. Help me to not get weary in well doing. Help to fix my eyes on you and seek your face. I thank you for knowing what's best for me. I thank you that your timing is perfect. Help me to not look at man's (Kronos) time but look at God's (Kairos) time. You are not slow to keep your promises. You will fulfill every promise in my life. I thank you for being patient with me. I thank you for not disqualifying me from the promise, despite my lack of faith. Help me to not rush, but to wait for your divine timing. In Jesus' mighty name, amen.

Day 30

Catch the Bouquet

"He makes everything beautiful in its time."

Ecclesiastes 3:11, NIV

I was walking out of the courthouse with my mom, my stepdad, my brother, and Nana. She had just gotten married to my stepdad, and we were walking towards the harbor. She had a beautiful bouquet full of red roses and gave them to me. I was walking down the street, recording on a mobile social media app, "I got the bouquet." At that time, I didn't understand the symbolism of why the brides throw the bouquet. I didn't know that it symbolizes who will be next to get married. I was 20 years old at that time and I wasn't thinking about marriage. I had been fascinated by the design of weddings and watched a celebrity wedding planner for inspiration.

Some of you have felt overlooked or forgotten by God. You may have seen many people get married before you; some that may have not desired it as much as you. However, it is your turn to catch the bouquet! In the right season, you will see why it may have taken longer than you hoped. God sees you, He knows your desires, and has not forgotten about you. Trust that in the right time, it will be your turn.

now

It's your time to shine!

Activation

Express to God how He is enough for you in this season. Esteem God and tell Him how much you love Him and how much you appreciate Him.

Reflect

Have you felt like God has forgotten or overlooked you regarding your marriage promise?

Have you found yourself envious at times of others getting married before you? If so, have you prayed about it and what did God say?

What would you want your wedding to look like? Think of who you would want to be there, colors, location, themes, etc.

What do you want your marriage to look like? What activities do you want to do with your future spouse? How do you want to feel when you are around your future spouse?

Pray

Father God, I thank you that you are making everything beautiful in its time. I thank you that you are connecting everything together for your purpose and glory in my life. I thank you that I'm not forgotten or overlooked. I thank you for preparing your best for me. Help me to not compare my journey with others. Help me to realize that if it hasn't happened yet, it just isn't time. Delay doesn't mean denial. You see and know everything, and you are shifting the proper things and people in place. Help me to not overly focus on the highlights of others or how long it's taking. Help to feel comfort knowing that my turn is coming, my name is being called, and my last name will change. I ask that you continue to help me focus on my assignments for now and continue to grow more intimate with you. In Jesus' mighty name, amen.

Closing Prayer

Father God, I thank you for those that completed this devotional journal and put in thought, time, care, and devotion into getting deeper intimacy and revelation from you. I ask that you illuminate different aspects of this devotional journal to them when they need it and remind them of what was written and the notes they have taken. May they look at how far they have come instead of how far they have to go. May they remember the Scriptures and hide your Word in their heart. Guard their hearts and minds in Christ Jesus. In Jesus' mighty name, amen.

Closing Encouragement

Thank you to everyone who read this devotional journal. I hope that this has encouraged you, inspired you, and to keep holding on to God's promises for your life. Thank you to my YouTube subscribers who have come across one of my videos and decided to purchase this. Thank you for supporting me and I'm grateful to have you as my subscribers. Thank you to some of my other friends I have met along this journey and have supported me. I'm going to leave you with this poem:

Crossroads Poem

by Janay Wells

Dear God, I'm at a crossroads. I'm not sure which way to turn
I know there are still many lessons I need to learn
God, please sharpen me so I know what to discern
You know my every thought before they are a concern
I'm walking and sometimes I feel lost, but I just keep walking

Dear God, I'm at a crossroads. I'm not sure which way to turn
I'm walking and talking to you Lord, show me where to go
I have made so much progress, look at me grow
You have paid the ultimate debt, there is nothing to owe
God you're shining on me, I have this Holy Spirit glow

Dear God, I'm at a crossroads. I'm not sure which way to turn
It is your will I am following, I'm trying to flow,
I don't want to be like the status quo

Sometimes it may take longer and feel like my journey is going slow
Weariness may set in, and I may start to feel low
I thank you God, you're putting on the best show

Dear God, I'm at a crossroads and now I'm certain which direction to go

Exclusive Encouragement

by Jeannette Bruno (beamyourlight)

A promise, a gift, and a blessing from our divine and true creator. Kingdom marriage is not only a covenant that the Holy Spirit births forth to bring love, hope, and daily sacrifice between a husband and a wife, but it is a perfect matrimony that allows two hearts to join in becoming one. What other God can do this?

I love this Scripture in Matthew 19:6 that says, "Therefore what God has joined together, let no one separate." When God brings his creation together for his wonderful and beautiful purpose, there may be trials and storms that try and wither his promises, but the beauty of His Word is that it shall come to pass.

Kingdom marriage is a beautiful moment, a pure timestamp, and the most perfect example of Christ and his bride. As we continue to see the Lord's hand in the royalty of what and who He brings together, let us acknowledge that God is the perfect creator, exquisite artist, and breathtaking promise maker. His beauty is splendid and honorable to all that wait before Him, honor Him, and show Him reverence within his grace.

Exclusive Encouragement

Dr. Rhonda Mayes

When we are waiting for the promises of God we often forget to simply sit at the feet of God. If you are in a season of waiting, the following Scripture will lead you and comfort you: “Wait on the Lord: be of good courage, and he shall strengthen thine heart: wait, I say, on the Lord,” (Psalm 27:14).

About the Author

Janay Wells is a graduate student studying mental health counseling, entrepreneur, author, and executive producer and talk show host of The Janay Wells Show. She dedicates her time to helping others overcome adversities. She is purpose-driven and passionate about sharing her story. She is the Chief Visionary Officer of Janay Cosmetics, a brand that ties together makeup and faith. She hopes to inspire other people to pursue Jesus and to follow their God-given purpose.

Contact

janaywells.com
weatherthewaitdevotional@gmail.com

Reach out to share testimonies, book speaking engagements, and more to weatherthewaitdevotional@gmail.com.

Join and Follow

Facebook: Weather the Wait: Journey to Kingdom Marriage

Instagram: @WeathertheWaitDevotional